Ikigai.

A reason for being; a reason to get up in the morning.

Just a Phase

The highs and down right lows of motherhood that people would quite frankly try to forget.

By Victoria Dos Santos

Copyright Pending
ISBN: 9798377873075

Dedication

For Doug, Emilia, and Bear because without you three I wouldn't be me. I dedicate this book to you.

Contents

Introduction 1
Phase one: It's a long one 2
Phase two: The arrival 7
Phase three: Feeding in the dark 9
Phase four: Sleep 11
Phase five: Holidays 13
Phase six: Weight 16
Phase seven: Food 18
Phase eight: Love 22
Phase nine: Witching hour 25
Phase ten: Weather 27
Phase eleven: Day trips 28
Phase twelve: Car seats 31
Phase thirteen: Teething, jabs and a crap day 33
Phase fourteen: A tidy house 35
Phase fifteen: Sensory classes 37
Phase sixteen: Screens 39
Phase seventeen: Getting older 41
Phase eighteen: Second Child Syndrome 43
Phase nineteen: The school run 47
Phase twenty: Going back to the grind (work) 50
Phase twenty-one: The gap 53
Phase twenty-two: Weekends 55
Phase twenty-three: Lie ins 60
Phase twenty-four: Getting your me back 62
Phase twenty-five: More food 65
Phase twenty-six: Traditions 67
Phase twenty-seven: Friends 70
Phase twenty-eight: When it's all said and done 72
Phase, oh who knows 79

Introduction

First, I want to start by saying that both my children have turned out very well. They are absolute legends and impress us every single day. I want to thank them for choosing me. I hope you can read my story, relate to it, laugh through it, but most importantly, I hope you find some comfort in the tales that so many of us don't want to share. Motherhood and all its trappings should be celebrated, so grab a glass and let's get started.

Oh, and I have broken this tale down into phases because let's face it, it's all a phase until it's not anymore.

Phase one: It's a long one!

2011.
The sweat was pouring off of me. For some reason, I had decided to walk from Whitechapel (East London) all the way home, which was not the best idea, seeing as the pavement was radiating heat and the sun was beating down on me, making me sweat like a pig. I had decided to walk, as the only other option was to vomit publicly on the tube roughly two stops away from home. It was in that moment I thought it may be a good idea to grab a pregnancy test and hope that what I pretty much knew was happening was a fact and not a figment of my imagination.

Before the phases all began.
When you meet a gorgeous, tall Brazilian man, you are a little star struck and end up making a total fool of yourself (more times than you would care to remember)! But, he stuck around and is still here to tell the tale along with me. However, this is not a love story, this is all the bits in between.

This book is about phase by damn phase all the raw, untold truths of parenthood. I don't claim to know everything, but I have been there, got the grubby t-shirt, and will share it with you—warts and all. So, if you are about to embark on the most radically life changing journey of your life or you are riding the wave headfirst, then sit back and find somewhere to hide, or wait until the cherubs are in bed and attack it then, this may take eternity to finish if you're anything like me and the moment they're in bed my battery is also about to die out.

My name's Victoria Dos Santos. Welcome to my parenthood adventure. Read along with me about the many highs and real fucking lows. I promise to make you laugh, if not with me, then at me, and I promise you I still don't have my shit together, even 11 years on.

Back to 2011.
The walk eventually gets me home. I grab the rectangular box from my bag and nervously stumble to the bathroom to do what needs to be done. The pee-sodden stick blurts back so innocently with a slight smirk to its two lined display. Victoria, you are bloody pregnant.

I want to make it perfectly clear that I understand whole-heartedly how lucky I am to be able to become pregnant, have a healthy pregnancy, a natural birth and a healthy baby at the end of it all. However, the overriding fear and emotion of being in charge of keeping another human alive apart from myself was a little too much to bare when it all became real. So, we ate pizza, watched something on T.V., and went to bed in our two-bed apartment in East London, a new world awaiting us only a Meer nine months away.

Nine months of renting my body out.
(If you loved your pregnancy, then you may want to skip this phase. If you were like me and struggled with every moment of it, then you may find some pleasure, or should I say pain, so please read on.)

I say this in jest, or do I? I envy you ladies out there that blossom at every trimester—skin glowing, sickness in check, and just kicking arse even while growing a tiny human. I, on the other hand, found the first trimester, or the first three months, exhausting, painful, nauseating, frustrating, more exhausting, and strange. Oh, how naive we were thinking this would be the most tired we could be! The sickness was unbearable, and many of my pleasures were taken away, like coffee, even the word would make me gag. Cupboards in our kitchen were sealed shut, and if anyone said "salmon," they better hope there's a bin nearby or else that vomit was coming straight for them.

The second trimester (4-6 months) was the best of the lot, a blossoming bundle of joy. My body, mainly my belly, decided to double in size, and from every angle, it looked like I was carrying more than just one in that tummy. There was a point in the pregnancy where my hips touched the sides of the bath, I kid you not. They were childbearing hips, getting ready for action from month four. I was still managing to cycle to work every day, dodging the daily traffic and red bus routes, so my hips must not have been as bad as I thought. I do vividly remember my nails being the healthiest part, dazzling with strength and vitality, while the rest of my body was inflated—left, right and centre.

Oh, and don't even get me started on the breast, nipple issue. My god, the pain! If you have ever experienced the first time your nipples become sensitised and fuller, then you will understand the unbelievable pain, especially on a cold day. No-one tells you about that. Or maybe, once we've had our baby, do we just forget about it all as we're so consumed by the next bloody hurdle that's being thrown at us?

What about patience? There's not much of that to go around when you're growing a human, as my work colleagues and anyone in close proximity could vouch for. As the third trimester rolled towards me so did the Autumn months. I found myself wanting to lie horizontally for longer periods of the day, even if it was on a few mats in the sports hall cupboard (I forgot to mention I'm a sports teacher) or passing out on the tube to find myself nuzzled on someone's shoulder doing the ever so graceful head nod back and forth. Sleep, rest, napping, siesta, or whatever you like to call it, I wanted it, and you could do nothing to stop me from having it. Moreover, pregnancy and body adaptations are happening day in and day out, and closing your eyes is overwhelming to say the least. So, we sleep, and I have never slept as well as I did during that pregnancy, waking up with a new lease of energy, to find it stolen within the first few minutes.

During the final trimester, when the Christmas build up was beginning, one day I managed to start a Christmas cake, clean the bathroom, tidy the cupboards, and wash and iron the baby clothes. In other words, I had begun nesting. Luckily, the distraction of Christmas, cooking, shopping, and wrapping took over, and before we knew it, Christmas Day was upon us.

I need to back track and mention this trimester took a turn for the worst, and sleep was few and far between. Watching the hunk sleep so soundly irritated the fuck out of me. "Good morning, darling. How did you sleep?" My response to this was usually minimal, but I believe my face said a lot more, kicking his arse into action and out of bed. Dear God, the lack of sleep—nobody mentions that you barely sleep in the final trimester. Nothing. Nada. Zilch. Oh, bloody hell!

Christmas Day.
Christmas lunch had completed, and gradually, the dull, period-like pains began. Slowly, oh so slowly, they increased with pain and frequency. I had a quick chat with my mum and the rest of my family who were in Devon. My Mum commented, "Oh, you're a long way off yet. You're still talking to us." What a lovely thought. But, as we know or may not know yet (which is the sweetest) when reading this, she was right about that pain, and it did get worse. With the 'pop' of my water breaking, I felt the crash, like a slap to the face, with the incredible sense of overwhelming pain and bewilderment of what was to come, oh the fucking pain!! (It needs all the exclamations, here's another one!)

The pain by now was something that can only be described as torture, wishing for that magic 10 to be mentioned. The hunk finally found a parking spot, arriving with jelly babies, lucozade, and then left again on a search for some way of playing the music we had selected, which by this point I didn't give a shit about! Oh, how naive we were!

Once inside the birthing room, which I must say was huge with a lovely big bath (NHS, we just got lucky), the time ticked on—1am, 2am… Oh, and as I had lost the will to speak, along with the need to be one of those legends, I decided to not have any pain relief apart from the gas and air, which when you are 8cm dilated doesn't do jack shit. Also, the man who had assisted in the procreation decided it was time for him to take a nap, and when it was time, he wanted to be woken up! For me, that most important person at that time was the midwife—she was all I cared about, my lifeline, my everything, until she buggered off to the loo and I found myself sucking on a canister of gas that didn't hit the spot. But we were nearly there, and the stunned superwoman (I shall call myself that I think, as we all should) had suddenly developed a mild roar that seemed fitting and would also ensure anyone in the room who was taking a nap wasn't anymore. And so, it began... the details we shall spare. Within what felt like forever but actually was just under an hour, our lives changed.

Phase two: The arrival

Off you go then! For me, the most bizarre part of becoming a parent is brutal reality and speediness of being quite literally shoved out of the hospital. It feels like you should be taking a test or saying an oath, but no. Within a few hours after the baby is checked, you are led out the door, complete with the stitches, pulsating boobs, and the terrifying thought of going for a wee or anything else at the back of your mind. You are left to your own devices.

I'll never forget that drive back home—cold, dark, and quiet. She slept beautifully, but all I could think about was what I would do when she wakes. These maternal instincts were definitely kicking in, along with the sadness of a life once had. Freedom and routine had always been a thing for me, and suddenly, all that was about to change. I had lost the control I took for granted or didn't know I had. No-one can prepare you for the sadness or loss for a life you used to have, even though the new life is even better. I just didn't know it for the first few months.

Once we got home, we settled into our first night of the unknown. We showered the Bub, spent an unhealthy amount of time changing the first nappy (I think it took around five minutes), ate something, and attempted to feed... Oh, dear God, breastfeeding. I don't know what your feelings are about this topic. I am on the fence. If you enjoy it and your baby latches, then I am all for it. But for me, this was not an easy and painless feat. The pain, even with help from midwives and family members just wouldn't disappear. My nipples were practically hanging off. We got to two weeks in, and I couldn't even express. The hunk decided to feed her, and I know, I know, but it was in the middle of the night, and he had no option but to give what he thought would be fine—your very own standard Sainsbury's whole milk. Well, that did not go down very well. Have you ever been so desperate for sleep you'd do anything? That was one of those moments, and there were a few more to come.

After that night, I gave in. It was two weeks after E's birth, and we switched to bottles. Thankfully, she took the bottle, as I'd heard so many horror stories from people in those chat forums telling of their baby not taking a bottle and being their only beck and call, without the help of anyone at any time. This worried me. On top of that, there was the constant worry of colic, washing, changing, changing myself, showering myself, dinner with the hunk, dinner with friends, reading, cleaning, and the list goes on. The first few months felt like a black hole—one that I may never get out of. I'll never forget when a friend said to me, "Don't you feel claustrophobic?" That one friend has three children now, but indeed, I did! I longed for this other life that no longer existed, and I wasn't sure when I'd feel normal again.

The days blurred and consisted of late-night drives to the supermarket, where I was quickly told by the hunk that the car wasn't parked straight. I, on the other hand, couldn't care less about this. I didn't care about much of anything then. So, into the supermarket we strolled. He needed the toilet and left me and the baby staring. Well, she couldn't even open her eyes really. I was staring at the yogurt, saying to myself: You'll be ok. He'll be back soon. Just being on my own was overwhelming, especially in a place I didn't want to be. Nowadays, I'll hide anywhere to get even two minutes to myself. He did come back, and off we went to buy the emergency formula that would be used after my boobs signed off to milking season—they were on strike! God, if only we could go on strike, what a world that would be. We shopped and headed home. This time, I didn't drive.

Putting the baby in the car, closing the door, and walking from their door to yours feels like freedom—or is it just me? For a few seconds, breathing in the air on your own, my God, those were the tiniest of moments I missed and longed for.

Phase three: Feeding in the dark

Feeding in the darkest moments of the night when you feel no-one else is awake can be a lonely point—oh God, such a lonely point—of the 24-hour cycle of early babyhood. Most of us know the evenings I'm talking about—the ones that stretch out into marathons of feed, sleep, dump, feed, sleep, dump, and that which the husband and I do not talk about—the witching hour which I think needs its own chapter!

Why doesn't anyone talk about this stuff? We silently struggle in the deepest, darkest of nights—when you crave the sun to come up just so you know the rest of the world is awake, and you're not on your own. I had joined some forums where we shared our horror stories through the night, and it was my absolute saving grace. We all lost touch the moment we could handle our shit, of course, but those ladies were my oracles, my saints in shining booby armour. Even with them though, I wanted to cry (and cry I did) anytime one or two would log off because their baby had finally crashed.

But morning always did come. Sometimes, the sun bloody shone and off we'd go. At this point, I craved other mums to hang around with, share and moan too. I wanted to walk in green fields and parks in East London, but for a lot of the time, the city only offered some of this, which was hard—really hard. So, it was no surprise to me that I quickly became friends with the barista who ran the church coffee shop. She made me laugh when I thought I had forgotten how to; she rocked the Bub so I could drink my coffee hot; She listened to me—someone who rarely shared much to anyone, especially about the struggles of my newfound motherhood. I want to say thank you; you don't know how much you helped me.

Moral of the story is... New mothers, talk to people. Don't sit alone. There are so many ways to be heard, and I promise you from the deepest, darkest moments of my time as a new mum, someone is always going to listen. Motherhood is a mess most of the time so try and embrace those high waves and ride the low ones, until you fall and land on a high one again.

New Year's Eve.
It was a week or so after the birth, and the hunk had to go to work. Being in the events industry, New Year's Eve is a pretty big one to miss. I made sure my friend stayed, so I wasn't alone. We celebrated with a bottle of cheap fix, and she tried to stay awake, but of course, she eventually fell asleep. Then, impending fear and anxiety in the pit of my stomach arrived. I'm alone, and this tiny human will wake soon, needing me and only me. Oh God, I just want to go back to before. I'm so lucky that this dull ache and resentment of everything prior disappeared; the utter enjoyment and exhaustion resumed.

But, nearly 11 years later, I will never forget how lonely I felt those first few months, when it felt like it was just me. Actually, in those darkest hours, it really was just me! If I can give one piece of advice, it would be this: believe in yourself. You can do this. You were meant to do this, and you will sleep again. You will be free to eat out again and drink a hot drink. You will. And it doesn't take long for it all to happen again. Normality (albeit a new normality) will seep in, and it is wonderful. But when you're looking at your bed, wondering when the next time will be when you can actually sleep in it again, uninterrupted it is all consuming. Those days were some of the toughest, but they become memories within time, and sleep does come back around again.

Phase four: Sleep

How did your baby sleep? In the beautiful artisan cradle you had handcrafted? The wicker rocking bed? Ours was the Pram. God, it felt like forever, but she did. In our room, she slept pretty well. Even though every time she moved, shuffled, or made a noise, I'd wake, at least some sort of sleep routine was kicking in. My mum was a strong believer in routine which was sometimes to our detriment (now I struggle to stay awake past 10pm). But in the early stages, her words were gospel and stamped forever in my brain, so off we went at six weeks old doing a top to tail in the evening to help with establishing that bedtime routine.

But no-one ever mentioned the fourth trimester. Anyone who out there who hasn't heard of this, you should see the shit show that unfolds in those early months. I worked hard on getting this routine in place at 6 weeks old, but every time I tried, I was reminded that she had no clue. She couldn't even really see me, but if she could, she'd be laughing at her poor mum slogging away to establish a rather fruitless routine. But I persevered anyway because there wasn't really much else going on to entertain me, so why not?

I love having routine in my professional life as a teacher. The chaos of craving for routine when you don't have it and can't understand when it will come back is tough. The juggle of managing to function on one hour of sleep, a baby who has decided they don't want to be put down, and trying to hold onto a marriage means that unless I'm superwoman, I cannot keep all those plates spinning without one of them coming crashing down. After four to five months, we did fall into a routine. There was a little evening that we were clawing back. We even managed to get into town for a lunch, which apparently I fell asleep at (not sure I believe this, but quite possibly true)! Have you ever had grand plans for something, but your child has other plans?

Phase five: Holidays

Eventually, the dreamy ideals of sitting by the pool sipping something cold while reading a trashy novel came to the forefront. *Sigh*, holiday. And so, discussions of Brazil and visiting the hunk's home country came to fruition. I had no idea, absolutely no idea what it was going to be like. The plan was for us to go to Brazil to introduce the Bub to the hunk's family and friends. The fact that I agreed to get on the plane without him is still a mystery to me, but I did and I'm thankful for this solo endeavour, it brought colour, passion and fire back into my soul.

Before getting on the plane, I forgot security would be questioning my six bottles of pre-made formula. The sheer volume I decided to take was another mystery to me, and then being asked to taste the white concoction was yet another. Have you ever tried formula? If you have, you'll understand what happened after my initial taste. As I moved to drink the second one, I felt my stomach switch, and throwing up was the only option. I moved as quickly as I could to the nearest bathroom, which was not that near and on the other side of security. For some reason, they allowed me through where I proceeded to throw myself on the toilet. The rest is history.

The Bub and I cautiously made our way back to security where they must have taken pity on me because they let me through. Alone with a night flight pending, I sat anxiously waiting to be called until a saving grace, who goes by the name of Enzo, invited us into the lounge where I drank three glasses of bloody good red and eased into the flow of travel. Until we needed to board the plane, the nerves set in. I had too many questions running through my head: Would she sleep? Will I be able to get her feed on the way up to avoid sore ears and her crying all flight? What will I do when I land? Will anyone speak my language? The anxiety was at sky level, so was the sweat. The attendant seemed to notice and took pity on me. She helped me get settled in—Bub on my knee with the most awkward baby belt strapped on. Then, off we went into the unknown, and my god it was the unknown.

Brazil.

We arrived, and I quickly realised no-one spoke bloody English. I had been oblivious to this fact. Trying to manoeuvre around an airport with basic Portuguese (and I mean basic) was a bloody mess! But the people of Brazil, the family and friends I made were the kindest, most fun and happiest hot-blooded individuals I've ever met. I was jetlagged and on the hunt for our friends who agreed to be my tour guides for the trip. The Bub was a bloody angel, but the aftereffects of the airport and plane drinking were starting to take their toll. All I wanted was a strong coffee and a lie down. No such luck!

Instead, I hauled the suitcases off the conveyor belt that secretly laughs at you as you struggle to run alongside the moving belt while your suitcase skims past. Doing this without leaving your child behind somewhere amongst the chaos is for another chapter. Eventually, we get the luggage (I'm not sure why I keep saying we, this is all me)! Then, off we go to find the hunks family and friends. The wonderful adventure about to begin.

Putting the sheer magnitude of the trip to the side, Brazil is one of the most beautiful countries I have ever been to, and the people are just fantastic. We stayed in Rio. Who doesn't love a cocktail while watching dancers in the back streets of Rio while the baby sleeps? This is what I signed up for all those weeks ago when I agreed to do this trip solo. To the bub- You will never know the amount of love and happiness you gave to so many people, in particular your Vova who showed you the bright lights of Brazil, the rocky mountains of Rio and the salty sands of Ipienema.

Brazil had many ups and downs, but it taught me to chill

out when it came to being a Mum. Also, sleep and routines! I did none of these. But I did manage to update my wardrobe, drink copious amounts of caipirinhas, and eat a lot of delicious food.

My takeaway: Go with the flow, relish every opportunity, and say yes! Your baby remembers nothing, but they can feel when the people they love so much are happy and content. Don't worry about routines, throw it out of the window, dance with strangers, drink fruity cocktails and watch the sunset and sunrise all in one night!

Phase six: Weight

Now I wasn't sure how to tackle this area, quite literally. For me, and as the wive's tale goes, breastfeeding shrinks you in a matter of weeks! Well, that myth stayed a myth for me because as you read before, breastfeeding and I did not get on well. To start with and during the latter parts of the pregnancy, I found it hard to fit into the bath. This is the honest truth. My hips were definitely built for childbirth. They expanded beyond belief, and I think would have kept on going had it not been for the baby making a swift exit. I digress.

Weight. And what to do with it? First, can I say embrace it! Your body has, in a matter of words, been rented out for the past nine months, and now that its shell is empty, it kind of likes the soft, squidgyness that the additional layers bestow. However, if you are anything like me and exercise has always been part of your daily life, then exercise is the vehicle to remove said excess squidge.

Exercise and the magic 'me time' that I coined in the latter stages of the Bub's first year, came from my innate need and desire to be ON MY OWN. This is part of my personality which I found to be more prevalent once I had a child that depended on me and me only. Daddy was there, but mum was the chosen one. For so many, this is the dream, and I get that! It's lush, but my God, how I fantasised about my own company. My time came when I took the tube to and from work, my 'me time' workout and the walk to and from the gym, and after bedtime. Those precious bedtime hours when it is just you, a glass (or bottle) of wine, and whatever your pleasure may be. I craved more and quickly realised that time was a "valuable commodity… value it accordingly. Never waste it away." —Matthew Dicks, who may be the one and only author I will recite. This idea is never so much at the forefront of anyone's mind other than a new parent, fighting for that freedom they flitted away all those years before.

So, exercise became my go to, to escape and be me—not mum, not wife, but me—and I savoured every moment. I became a leaner version of myself—at times too lean, but don't you worry, those cheat meals soon became cheat days, and the weight my body craved like I did for 'me time' crept back on. I would make it a point to look in the mirror and thank my body for what it has done for me in my life. I have been very lucky. I didn't really struggle weight wise, I never broke a bone, and I managed to house babies for nine months without any help. These things are miracles, and the older I get, I realise exercise should be to take care of said body, nourish it, thank it, and be grateful for it. I have no other body, and quite frankly, I don't want another. All I do want is my time to sit and do whatever I want for days upon end and not feel so damn guilty for it! We will get into mum guilt a little later, but what the hell is that all about anyway?

Make exercise something that gives you joy. Your body has gone through a transformative stage, and to be honest, it's badass and continues to only get better with age. So, embrace it and understand all that it does to serve you every single day! It took me quite some time to thank my body for enabling me to sit at my husband's desk right now at 6:03am and write this passage to you now. No pain, no sadness, just utter gratefulness for all that I am. So, please do one thing today, celebrate you and all that you are now and will be.

Phase seven: Food

Food. Glorious food.
Oh, how I devoured the carbs through pregnancy, ate my way through stacks of salted peanuts during my rough attempt at breastfeeding, and would splurge during the wee hours of the morning. Who doesn't love a wedge of cheese and tiger bread at 3am? The tales you are told during the early stages of motherhood are insane. We've all heard them. They tell us about what we should and shouldn't eat. Or they'll say if you look at a beige piece of bread or attempt to dunk a beige biscuit in your morning coffee, then you will be destroying the human you have just brought into the world and will go to hell. God help us all, that we have a brain cell or two between us and realise that the myths of years past are not true, that everything in moderation is a life well lived and that's really all that matters.

Take eating out before children and eating out with. The speed eaters have nothing on a woman trying to eat before her baby wakes, moves, or wails for her attention. To this day, I eat so much more quickly than I should, getting ready for the next child tantrum or growl for momma attention. Each day hails the question: will the food I eat and the drinks I drink be at my own pace or at the boss of the house's speed? Answers on a postcode. The relationship between food, time, and enjoyment are in three different universes, and I strive to unite all three one day to enjoy a meal in peace, on my own, savouring every last minute with a glass of red and a book by my side. Pure bliss! Let's break down the three main meals of the day, and please nod when you agree.

Breakfast, also known as breaking the fast, in the early stages of motherhood would have been taken in the wee hours of the morning, for me at least. So really, this meal is a kind of brunch, but not those lavish brunches. A kind of breakfast that I may get to sit down and eat, or I may not. I am a breakfast person. I love it. I love all it symbolises and yearn for what it used to be and will become again. A big spread for all to enjoy, especially on the weekends, is a pleasure that I hope is had by all with the blaring Peppa Pig monologues going on in the background.

The iPad was my saviour during the early stages of introducing food to the baby. She would zone out, and I could feed her anything and everything and she would consume it (judge me all you like). If there is a way to feed, shower, read, and take a breath, the screen will be used, and I have no problem with that. The people that wince and say I would never do that are lying! I just know it. We do what we do to get through the day. The rest is history.

Lunchtime is here, and it is normally somewhere near a park if the weather is kind. Otherwise, this meal is usually at home, grazing on the baby's leftovers. My word, she eats well. I think one of the first things I pureed and froze was a banana parfait. I soon decided that she just needed to eat what we ate with a lot less salt. Food for the little one was never an issue and became three square meals for me too. The hours around these three moments was the issue, especially when she started to sleep more at night and a routine was established. The glass of wine or two and the cheese and biscuits or bag of chocolate would come out, and everything else was just noise. What is it about sitting down on your own to watch some shit on TV that leads to the sudden urge to be accompanied by some other type of shit... carbs! And not the good stuff. The better she slept, the more I would eat and snack and eat and snack. This continued for several weeks until I started to read, study, and fill my brain with things other than baby stuff. Learning about glucose spikes, the hungry hormone, and the 'I'm full up hormone,' I realised that eating at such times of night was doing serious damage to my insides and that was enough for me to cut the binge. Instead of eating the stuff, I started to make and bake. Until The Great British Bake Off finished and all normality resumed, I blame the carb binges on that bloody programme. Is there anyone that ends watching that show not running for the biscuits and crisps? If not, you're a stronger woman than I am!

While we're on the subject, what's your go-to snack? Or something you love to indulge in? Mine would be a Saturday or Sunday morning croissant and coffee, not just one. Normally, there's two to three consumed, especially if the hunk has taken the baby out for a walk, and I can eat alone. Otherwise, it is eaten in between getting up and sorting someone else out. Having a little French blood in me has always driven me towards those butter laden delicacies,. Actually, I'm off to get one now.

Dinner time could go one of two ways—eating like a gannet or eating leftovers. I love a bloody good feast. But it's having the energy to cook it and sit and eat, especially when the hunk is normally out in the evening, working. We are left to sort ourselves out, speaking as if my daughter can actually fend for herself. Mumma's got it, and she'll make sure we're all fed and watered, don't you worry.

Who loves to cook here? See, I do, and I have a dreamy idea of how I want to cook. I am in my Italian kitchen with an array of vegetables, a glass of wine in hand, and music blaring. Children are playing harmoniously in the background. The husband is relaxing, and all is calm. Switch to reality—we're in our then two-bedroom apartment with what seems to be an afterthought of a kitchen. The Italian, rustic escape is nothing but a lucid fantasy! But I bet you your bottom dollar I'll be doing a Nancy Silverton during my weekends away before you know it. Everything is possible, and if the want is big enough, it will come true. Well, that's what I tell myself as I type this away in the hunk's office.

When it comes to food, we must dream big. My background is in health. I love it, I really do, but I would say only in the last few years has my interest turned into a passion. I can now spend time, 10 minutes here and there studying and reading what I love, and cookbooks! The bread baking has become my fascination. I will bake the perfect sourdough; it just hasn't happened yet. You can probably tell as I'm writing this all my shit has come together and that 29-year-old is a distant memory—the girl that became the woman in a space of a few months. Yep, this is true. But my God, the love of food, good stodgy food is still there and comes to the forefront every once in a while. But now, being 39 and, if I want it, I eat it. Now I care about the health of my body. I understand if I eat that freshly baked cinnamon bun cake, I now understand that everything I eat has a repercussion, and that's all good, it really is all good.

So, binge at 3am. If that puts a smile on your face, lick on an ice cream, chomp on some damn good pasta, and feast on a bag of sweets, because believe me, your body is forgiving and sometimes the only comfort and glimmer of hope to get us through the day in those dark, cold, wet, and windy days is some good, wholesome bag of crap. You are all very welcome, and never ever let anyone say otherwise.

Phase eight: Love

The love you have for each other before and after a child changes dramatically. My story may be different from others as the hunk, and I only met a few months before the baby was conceived. Barely knowing each other, and as we know within a few months we made a human. In all my 28 years, I did not know that making a human would be so quick and easy. But knowing and seeing what I have now ten years on, we were and are very fortunate indeed to be able to create humans so easily. I just have to look at the Brazilian stallion and I feel the rumbling of a newborn in the pit of my uterus! Children had never been on my radar, so I hadn't really given it much thought, but he had and when I announced it to him, the look in his eye shifted. The sheer relief that his swimmers swam where they should and reached the finish line with no hiccups was really what he had been seeking all this time.

I find the word love and everything it is entangled within confusing and strange. Being a mother, I clearly know what love is for my child. I would happily walk in front of a bus for her and not think anything of it, but for him, ooh now that would need some thinking over. I know I would contemplate walking near the bus, but actually putting myself in front of it is a whole new ball game. And one I'm not sure I would be happy to play. But, ask me if I love him, oh absolutely. Is that tangled up in the love I have for my children? Again, absolutely. But does he look damn sexy 10 years on? Hell yeah!

There have been many highs and lows in our love during these 11 years. At times, he's screamed at me. He'll hate me for saying this, but the Brazilian blood runs deep. The blow outs have been real, the walk outs again real, and I've happily slammed the door behind him. The embracement of friends and family members I cannot communicate with has been one of the realist and most bizarre things I've been a part of. Born and raised in the UK, I had not come up against any language barrier until the hunk came along and so did his family and friends who opened their arms to me and all my trappings. I know if we shared the same language, they would for sure prefer my banter over his rather questionable funny side. But when you love someone, the language barrier, which is a rather huge barrier along with the cultural differences of growing up in countries and families of hugely contrasting beliefs, characteristics and journeys. You realise that none of that matters when a child comes into the world. All anyone cares about is them, the rest is just noise. You come together and work through it. Fortunately for me, the hunk speaks better English than me, which can be a positive and sometimes a negative.

Finding that time for us to just be us as you know was very much nonexistent. When family were around (mainly the hunks family) we were free as birds physically to do and please as we wished, mentally I found that tough to walk out the door and leave my pride and joy- the Bub behind, but listen to me. You must, must must remember why you chose each other in the first place, rebuild, rejuvenate that love again for each other, as we all know it becomes lost when you bring a human into the world. A lot of the time we were riding solo and navigating that rocky path together. We became regular dine in takeaway fiends at times, getting to know the local delivery takeouts by first name. The Bub somehow out of nowhere slept pretty much through the night from well beyond her first birthday. I would like you to know this was based on filling her up just before bed with a bottle of milk (formula, guys) and making sure her daytime naps didn't end too closely to the witching hours (more of that to come). With a routine beginning to take shape, we had grand plans for marathon movie nights, long dinners and a. It of how's your father. Instead, what did we do with that time? Of course, the only thing new parents would do: sleep. Getting into bed and enjoying the shut eye that we both needed so so much. Discussions of a holiday together without the baby were also on the cards and how we missed just being us. Most of the time, we were the B team, and the human next door who had no idea what was going on was A team, a team of her very own.

Moreover, I have been trying to rack my brain to figure out how to describe the relationship, love for each other, and how it became over the space of a night very different. They said it wouldn't last, that it was all about the looks and the desire. We are older and wiser now, growing wiser to being able to switch each other off when the other one has too much to say, comes with a mature relationship. Looking back on the first year or so of parenthood, we didn't have a clue, but we muddled through, and that human is still thriving today! So, we didn't do too bad my hunk.

As I've mentioned before I'm set in my ways, a bit of a loner, an introvert with an extroverted job. I'm confusing to many and a good ole laugh to some. How this personality of type A-Z works in a relationship is bewildering. I am the most laid-back partner going, which of course is a great thing, but at times, it can be taxing and confusing. Not just for the receiver. I have a feeling my offspring have taken on some of these peculiar traits. I love to be wanted, but as we know being parents, you are wanted all the time. A love you can't say no to, but my God, all you want to say is piss off and leave me alone. Actually, don't leave me alone, stay with me. No, piss off. I want me time. I feel guilty for me time. You're the best. You're so annoying, frustrating. God, I'm the worst. Those mental breakdowns can happen whilst I walk to the bloody gym. I mean, come on! Finding the balance, of wanting to be needed and wanting to be alone is a balance I still don't have the answer to, I'll let you know if I ever do.

Phase nine: Witching hour

In my early thirties, I hadn't ever thought about meditation, breath work, stretching, or things along those lines. Controlling my thoughts has only just come in recently as I veer headfirst into my forties. But don't forget, I love love this human and would do anything at any time for said baby. But my God, I'm going to say it, and come on, you can too. For me, some of my best parts of the days are when I creep out of said baby's bedroom, retreat to the sofa, stick on some shit TV, and down a few glasses of the good stuff. Hell to the yea! Another day done, and I am finally on my own in my happy space, holding onto the night for at least the next two glasses of vino.

Welcome to the witching hour.
Well, no-one tells you about this bloody monstrosity, do they? The hour/s are utter bullshit. The hour can be afternoons, mornings, evenings, weeks, or pure unadulterated hell. Where there can be constant screaming, attachment issues. That's just from the parent who is in the mix of it, and I have to say it is normally just one of us, unless you are lucky enough to have two adults at home who can share the wonder that is the witching torture. I had heard of rumblings of said witch but didn't quite understand it, which was a blessing. I think less of us would procreate if we understood that the human we gave birth to could turn into a human from hell in the span of a few seconds. I experienced all manner of witching madness. From days on end, going to the loo meant she was lying or sitting on one knee. Putting her down was out of the question, and of course, only momma could soothe such ailments. When there is no temperature, teething, hunger, or pain to throw the

madness at, you begin to question your sanity and that of your neighbours who may be home and willing to watch over said human so you can use the bathroom in peace.

I think we can consider these days, weeks, months as phases. Dear God, who invented the phases chat? Where we simply boil everything down to: it's just a phase. When you're in it, it bloody doesn't feel like a phase, it feels like an eternity of ground hog day madness! And then you're out of it. They'll go down without screaming. They'll sleep again through the night. Those days do come back around again, but for some, that can take what feels like a lifetime. My little piece of advice—when you're out of the madness, try not to rub that into your friends face who is evidently still in the black hole somewhere trying to come up for a sliver of light. Sometimes, just offering a moment for them to grab a shower, drink a hot drink, or whine to you without you saying anything is all they need at that moment in time.

I have wallowed in my self pity, envious of life going on outside of my four walls. Looking back so many years later, those times were such small blips, but if I could have run away at moments or screamed from the roof tops, I would have done so in a heartbeat. Once again though, the moment when they fall asleep and complete peace overrides all, you forget all that came before and miss them, but never enough to dare to wake them, that would be sacrilege.

Phase ten: Weather

The weather now plays a huge factor in the planning of life outside of the four walls. And coming from the UK, there really is planning involved. In the early stages of parenthood, we were lucky to leave the house before 11am. The task of leaving the house that was once a matter of zipping up, drinking up, and leaving with a smile, would now be a military operation. Going to the local park, getting the car…oh, the bloody car. The car seat is a whole other discussion. The clothing that needs to be planned and spares that need to be packed, just in case of all weather eventualities all must be planned for. But hey, who actually wants to spend too much time discussing the weather? Well, the English do, that's for sure. They love to chat about all things sun, rain, and cloud. But let's not waste anymore of our precious time discussing the things out of our control. Just don't forget to pack the night before and have a little changeable bag ready to go by the door to avoid forgetting the morning of. Your future self will be grateful.

Phase eleven: Day trips

I think this section flows quite nicely. A day trip can be as easy as pie if you plan and get some stuff packed the night before. But who actually has the energy to pack, plan and be ready the night before, we all prefer to run around like a scene from home Alone the morning of said day trip. I'm saying this now, planning to get out and about the morning of, and I will without a doubt forget something. That goes without saying. So, I generally will have a set bag for days out ready to go. I have this all now because I am not knee deep anymore in nappies, formula and everything else. However, this morning I had an internal melt down (half term) and wanted to escape my current family set up and run away. The hunk happily said he would 'help out,' but seeing as he's just come back from knee surgery and my mum guilt kicked in, I of course said don't worry, you get going. I've got it covered. What is that about? Why don't we just say yes, thanks, and see ya, rather than ensure all meals are taken care of and a day bag is set by the door with snacks and everything else provided? If we are going on a day trip as a family, the hunk will simply say we're going and expects everyone to be ready in the car by the time he's finished his second or third toilet break. Oh, and he's at it again as I type this!

Let's reverse back to the days when we, I mean I would summon up the courage to leave the apartment to nip to Tescos to grab God knows what, probably some more wine. This is a walk a few minutes down the road, but the moment we left the apartment, got in the lift, and headed out, there would be a squeal from the concealed walls of the pram. I would ignore it and hope it would dial down. Sometimes it would, and sometimes it would not. I would simply turn around and go back into the sanctuary of my four walls. Back then, getting things delivered was a bloody chore, and the days of convenience were only beginning to emerge. Day trips were to the park at the end of our road.

These were dark days. Freedom was well away from me, and those days when there was literally nothing to look forward to were the toughest and loneliest I ever experienced. But these were days I wish I knew what I know now and opened up a book and studied or just escaped into a land somewhere else. I got my itch back for reading and the love to learn, in my mid-thirties, and as you may remember, the Bub entered my life in my late twenties.

Back to day trips, travelling across London would equate to that and the invitation (albeit a mandatory one) to go back into work and have my back-to-work meeting was an epic journey I still remember vividly today. Of course, the drive into North London from East London was fine, strapped into the car seat like a dream, milk fed and off she went to the land of nod. You know where this is going. The catch up and hellos and goodbyes with colleagues was a breeze, and then, the journey back home just before rush hour. I thought I'd nailed the trip, sitting there smug as they come I can do this.

The tiny human in the back had other plans for her overconfident mother. On the third red traffic light (of course), she whimpers and whimpers again. I haphazardly try and comfort her through the weird back seat mirror and try to pet her, from my front seat. On traffic light four, she erupts, like a revving engine dialed up. And of course, it's gridlock, nowhere to stop, music doesn't sound it out. Now, I know many of you will sympathise with me here and relate. Some, and I need to be the second set of you, where you comfort, keep calm, and know that all will be fine. Not for me. I stop the car right next to a KFC double red lines, take her out of the car seat as she's losing all colour from her face, and jump into KFC. I calm her and myself down with a toilet break, with her on my knee and a cuddle, of course. She's fine, so we walk out of KFC to see my sodding car being lifted onto a truck to be taken to the pound. No way! I cry out to the guy doing just this, and he looks at me and carries on. I turn around and three students I used to teach call my name. Now, these were the kind of students that would have hurled a chair at me a year ago. They saw I was in no joking mood, ran over, spoke to the driver for what felt like forever, and a miracle happened. My car was dropped (yep, dropped) to the ground, gave me a ticking off, and left as quickly as they'd arrived. The kids who saved me got a KFC out of it. I took a deep breath, popped her into the car seat, shut the door and prayed we would get home in one piece.

I live to tell the tale today, but when you're in it and they are just not playing ball, there is simply only one thing you can do: make sure they have a fresh nappy, they are fed, and you pray to the higher gods it's your day.

Day trips became trips around our development, holidays and trips to North London were postponed until she could count to 10.

Phase twelve: Car seats

Before we get started here, can we all think back to when we were babies? Yep, I just said that. Now, you may be younger or older, but hopefully, you can relate to the following. I sat on my mum's knee during any car trip we went on, and I must say they were few and far between, but there was definitely no baby seat and absolutely no Isofix. We survived. I'm not advocating we all ditch the car seat and go old school, I'm just saying.

We went all out and got the best reviewed car seat and Isofix. The hunk loves a review and will spend quite some time reading through a set of reviews. So, after spending some serious money on said car seat, which I know is worth every penny, did she go happily go in the car seat? Jesus, no. She would scream it out. Until one day, I stuck a coloured picture from Google on the back seat where she faced, and bobs your uncle, she sat. I mean not forever, but long enough to get to where we needed to go, which actually was just the local Brazilian restaurant. She would store every biscuit, cracker she could, somewhere in that seat, so any chance of us selling that seat at the end of it was a definite no. Moreover, the wet wipes came to the rescue again with a wipe over and good as new. What would we do without a set of wet wipes at our disposal? Even to this day, I'll have some stashed away just in case!

Prams, buggies, strollers, whatever we call them are our saviours, and quite frankly a mobile carrier for all the shit we decide to take with us. We went for a pram after seeing our friends spend the best part of 15 minutes trying to get their pram into the boot. We decided to keep it easy, and with one click, and fold we were good to go.

Let's talk about status and why oh, why do we add more

drama to our lives by adding a pram to the whole status scene? You know the prams I mean. If there is one thing I have learnt, it is that we should never ever subject ourselves to spending hundreds and hundreds of pounds on something that they will ultimately grow out of. Of course, we won't mention any brands, but know how much you spent on basically a wheelie bin for yours and your child's crap to be stored. And don't get me started on the newborn pram, which in a matter of a few months needs to be replaced with the second purchase: the toddler seat. Those companies are onto a bloody good thing.

Saying all this, I still could never get my brain around the swaddling or wrap around the body contraptions and just how it all worked. I wish I did, especially when all I needed to do was hoover and that free hand would have come in very handy. A pram is a pram and if you can afford it, well who am I to get in your way. At the end of the day get one with big wheels, folds easily and keeps the sun out of their eyes, if you tick all those boxes, then that's money well spent, whatever your budget maybe.

Phase thirteen: Teething, jabs and a crap day

What a phase.
Let's just tackle it all together and not spend too long on all of this. Let me put this bluntly: they need teeth. It's going to happen, so we just need to get through it. The first cut is always the deepest (sorry couldn't resist). But it is the toughest. When you break it down, it's pretty savage what's going on there and bloody painful. If I could give you a magic potion to tell you how you can sail through it, I'd be on my own private beach now sipping on a glass of fizz and whispering sweet nothings to the hunk, but I don't. When it begins—you know, the endless drool and clinginess begins—know there is an end to this. Yep, there are some tough nights ahead, but try to embrace it, and "this too shall pass." Abraham Lincoln.

Give them all the cooling tools they need to chomp on. I would dab a little olive oil with oregano (the tiniest amount, I am not a Doctor so please consult first before applying.) onto her gum which would help at times to soothe her. The colds and sleepless nights are the toughest. When you feel everyone else is asleep and you are the only one awake, please rest assured you are not the only one awake - there are so many of us joining you in this uphill climb. You've got this, the next tooth come along a lot easier. I promise you that. I will keep coming back to this: you are not alone. You will never be alone. Take solace and strength in that. You are given what you can overcome, and you will overcome the lows, but when they come (and they do in a huge crashing wave), celebrate those highs with every ounce in you. I keep saying this, but it bares repeating.

Right back to it, jabs seem to never end in that first year.

Just the getting to the surgery was a bloody effort—feeding, dressing, and getting out the door for the vaccinations in those first few months were incredibly challenging, and my surgery was at the end of the road. A little trick I picked up from one of the mums on some random group I'd started stalking late one night—take a bottle or whip the boob out during and after for a swift and seamless end to what feels like a never ending stream of needles. For me, the second set of jabs when your child is old enough to know you're mummy and that you will never let anything hurt them is like pure torture. As they're staring up at you and in goes the first of three jabs, there's nothing you can do apart from trying not to weep. Some of us have a midwife we would like to take home with us, and some of us including myself have what best describes this excuse of a midwife, who will happily stab a few needles into unsuspecting infants any time of the day. She reminded me very much of Aunt Trunchball from that well known book.

Phase fourteen: A tidy house

Is it really worth it?
This is the million-dollar question. My memories of childhood include a lot of my mum tidying and keeping the house clean for the unsuspecting visitors that would drop in. Did they care? Probably not, but that didn't matter. I carried a little of this with me, and I thought at times a tidy house was a measure of how well I was coping. I can't lie, I do like a tidy house, but a lived in one, nonetheless, where the toys are splayed about, evidence of a good living been had is all to see. A house where guests don't worry about where to sit or worry to ask for a cup of tea as it may mess up the kitchen. Nope, not for me. My house is your house, and my fridge is always wide open, just don't forget to make me a cup while you're at it.

The hunk is a whole other species. Buttering a piece of toast, I turn around to use said knife to spread the marmite and that knife is already making its way to the dishwasher or sink, or near that area. Apparently, I mentioned that I liked things put in the dishwasher a certain way, and since then, he has decorated the areas near the dishwasher with dirty crockery waiting for the mystery dishwasher cleaner to magic them away.

Clothes are another thing. They never quite make the laundry basket, decorating the surrounding areas instead. Dear God, am I the only one? Or is this a common occurrence where the magic tidy up fairy (AKA me) goes around and tidies up after said human? But a tidy house, is sometimes an unhappy house. Remember the plates will get cleaned, the laundry will get washed and the dirty marks will be wiped away. But the little people making those marks will grow and won't always be there to make a busy, messy house, so embrace the chaos and just side eye your hunk and hopefully he'll get the message. There are many ways that message can be sent, if you catch my drift!

Phase fifteen: Sensory classes

This all pisses me off. I am trying to prevent myself from going off on a rant, but why oh, why do we compete against one another over such silly unimportant things? The first class I went to was a sensory/nursery rhymes session in a lovely leafy part of east London. The after chat got my goat up, and I swore never to go back again. I didn't, and shockingly, my child seems to be fine, even though I didn't breastfeed her for years on end, swaddle her to sleep, and give her only organic food forever more. The real issue for me was the sleep conversation again—the women and men that would boast about their child sleeping through the night and never ever using a screen or any such device to allow them a minute or two. Utter bullshit and so fucking boring. Does it help anyone to know that your child sleeps through the night (which at four months I doubt) or that you can meditate and get your work done uninterrupted? Nope, no-one needs to hear this. Well, I certainly did not.

I'm a realist. Yep, there were weeks where we would get wonderful hours upon hours of sleep, and there were months where we didn't because I was sick or she was sick or the hunk had man flu, and the screens were used just to get through an hour of recovery. The food we ate wasn't always organic, pesticide-free, or the colours of the rainbow. There were freezer dinners happening where anything from the freezer would do because life got in the way, and sometimes, I just didn't fancy getting off the sofa to do any more than stick a pizza in the oven. As I said before, we have all survived unscathed and surprisingly in one piece.

Be a supporter. Don't gloat if it's not being asked for. Find solace and peace with others and not an excuse to shout from the heavens all your successes. Sometimes it's not needed; you just need to read the room before opening up.

Phase sixteen: Screens

I think we have led nicely into this topic. What an interesting topic it is, and could it be any more controversial? I have a love-hate relationship with devices. The sometimes educational content watched has been a life changer. However, flip the coin and my child would much prefer to watch someone painting their nails or unwrapping a random and useless toy which then she demands she needs in her life. This sort of free childcare I can deal with for short periods of time. My conscience and mum who gives a shit brain kicks in and understands fully what is being observed is adding absolutely nothing to my child's life, but am I sipping on my hot coffee in peace? Am I typing away here uninterrupted? Yes, all because of said YouTube I totally disagree with but love at the same time.

But really, they shouldn't be educationally stimulated 24/7. Sometimes, they need to escape and get time on their own, and who am I to judge what it is they watch? As long as it isn't harming them in the long run, I need to be ok with it. My sister once said to me: What's the deal with parents and kids on devices? I asked what she meant by this, and she simply replied, "Well, aren't you always on your phone? Isn't the world run by technology? They will grow up using tech. Why do we have such a problem with it when they're at home?" In a roundabout way, this is true and beating ourselves up about it really isn't the way to go. My then Bub is now turning 11 and a bloody clever cookie. Did she watch a load of unwrapping of toys and cutting of slime objects? Yes, she did, but she turned out a pretty rounded gal, so we'll leave it there I think.

All day, every day I have a problem with, but will I be the one who has devices on the table at the restaurant so myself and the hunk can eat in peace? Yes, I will. And I'll raise a glass to the rest of you doing that too. Eating dinner in peace whilst on holiday is a must. I haven't spent all that money so I can stand knee deep in a pool all day and sit down to a buffet extravaganza with a moaning Minnie next to me. The device with the headphones will be handed over and enough of that. I hear the other side of the coin—the parents who are stuck in the 80's and not succumbing to the device game. I see you, I raise a glass to you, and I hear you, normally a few decibels too high as you try to play a stimulating game of Uno across the table in a family packed restaurant or a game of rhetoric or two. We'll join you at the beach with a hangover after too many uninterrupted all you can drink sugar tails **AKA** momma cocktails!

Phase seventeen: Getting older

This could go two ways. Over the past few years as I've approached my forties, the thought of getting older and preparing for said oldness has become more of a common thread in my thoughts. Do we have savings? Do we have enough pots of savings? Should we put more money away? Oh shit, we have none. What are we going to do? What happened to turning 40 and retiring? The panic sometimes sets in, but before I delve too deeply into this convo, can we chat about our babies growing up?

Now, you may be reading this holding your first born who has just arrived into the world, or you maybe, like me, have one child turning 11 and a second child (who has yet to be mentioned but will be mentioned a hell of a lot more in pages to come) is turning six. See, it can't all be that bad if we forget the first few months of pure madness and have more tiny things to keep up with, giving us more work to do. Let's get things straight. They grow up, and sometimes the days feel like a series of groundhog days that will never end, but speak to a parent that sends their child off for their first day of school. They will resonate with the following: Time has never gone so fast, the moment they walk through those school gates for the first time. You ultimately measure the year within the constraints of the academic calendar, be it the state system where your child will have roughly 13 weeks off a year or the private system where it feels as if you are paying for them to be on holiday! No matter where or how you choose to educate your child, the moment they begin it seems as though someone pressed fast forward in life and you sometimes (only sometimes) wish for those long, endless days of nothingness where you could stay in all day watch episode upon episode of junk as your tiny human fed and slept, would return.

The grass isn't always greener. This is a saying I think so many of us take throughout life. Looking over the fence, listening into a conversation, scrolling through a more glamorous life, listening to our friends and their stories of their grown-up children and how they have their lives back again. I think we can safely say we've all done this and wished for another life, or variation of ours, with rose tinted glasses. Looking back now with an older and slightly wiser head on my shoulders, I feel my life with its ups and downs has been damn good, a lot of that is to do with the one constant in my life- the hunk, thank you. I don't wish for something else. I don't look to be more or less of what I am. All I strive for each day is to give my children strong foundations as they make their way through life.

They are growing up and so am I. Only in the last few years has that reality as I said earlier come to pass. Time is forever moving. We are forever evolving for good or for worse. They will grow, and I am making a point now of getting some of my life back, so I have an identity when they start to live theirs. Live in the present, as much as you can. I know the days are long and the years are short, but they really are no matter what stage you are in.

It can be hard to believe when you are in the thick of things—dishwasher going, clothes that need washing, folding, forget the ironing unless you really need to! Life is happening right now as you read this page, what is surrounding you? Is it a life you dreamed of (and I don't mean unicorns and cupcakes), a life full of life, warts and all? If so, enjoy it. Stop and watch it unfold because it unfolds faster than you or I could ever imagine!

Phase eighteen: Second Child Syndrome

Enter my wild child.
If she can do it, so can I. Welcome to Bear's world. Things started to come a little quiet in our household around the time the Bub became four. So, we decided let's try and add another into the mix. Bear in mind, we weren't being asked to give her a sibling. It was purely we should and so we would. As I have mentioned before, we are in the incredibly fortunate tribe of being able to put this plan in motion and stars align, nine months later there's another one. We are blessed. Due to the fact that our first child's behaviour was predictable, tantrums few and far between, sleep patterns easily constructed, eating and sleeping was dreamy, we had a feeling were in for it with the second.

Welcome Bear, who roared into our lives within 20 minutes of my waters breaking. She hung around in that cosy cocoon for longer than I would have wanted (2 weeks to be precise), and as you may remember, I'm not a mad fan of renting out my body for nine months. The moment the contractions came flying in from 0-100 in a space of seconds, I knew we were in for it. This all being said, the room we had been given looked like something you'd pay serious money for at a five-star hotel. We did not pay any money but seemed to have the ward to ourselves, along with a ginormous bath that I decided to stay in. Gas and air once again made an appearance, jelly babies and lucozade this time, and an understanding of the ring off fire I braced myself. She came pounding in through the ring of fire that to this day sends chills through my body, even five years later. People forget to mention the sheer brutality of childbirth and the exhaustion. We must never forget that prior to this baby coming into the world, we have just been through several months of anguish, anxiety, self-loathing, exhalation, joy, and barely any shut eye.

High on adrenaline, a human is handed to us, and we are pretty much told to get packing. Let's not forget the miracle that has just taken place, let's take a moment to celebrate this. However your baby entered the world, they entered and that is thanks to you and the wonderful home you gave it to grow and prosper. The next phase of getting out of the hospital and home happens for too quickly for many of us, support and real guidance of the next steps must be readily available when the mother needs. Do not be afraid to ask and ask again and again when you need that reassurance.

Instead, we are handed a baby said well done, then immediately put into a state of panic if we don't get our baby to latch onto those monstrous nipples we must be failing. You are not.

In all of this our second child had arrived and it's true what they say—the excitement for the second is just as much; however, you do leave the hospital feeling like you've got this, how can it be, we've done this once, we of course can do it again. Leave it with me!

Famous last words.

We had moved homes to a more leafy and safer part of the world. With the new baby in tow, we headed for home to begin the next chapter of parenthood. This time, I have raging hormones that are different than before. They are understood, yet different, and they all circle around the other child, the obsessive mother I am and wanting to hold onto things before, so yep, the first day back I decide everything is normal. The Bear (her nickname, that sums up our second child) is sleeping, so I'll walk my big girl to school, five minutes down the road. What could possibly go wrong? Lesson learnt. Within minutes of catching up with the mums at drop off, there's a message and voice note pinging, "Get home. She needs feeding, and I can't bloody do it." One day after giving birth, I leg it back home, whip out the boobs, and seal the hunger deal. Lesson learnt, until the formula comes along!

Bear latched and fed well. My anxiety and constant nerves were much less which helped immensely. The days passed with a sense of calmness. The gradual buildup of worry would be surrounding the school pick up and if she would need feeding, would she start screaming? Would she be asleep when we needed to leave the house? Would she need a nappy change just as we're about to leave? I guarantee that.

Another thing people don't discuss is the jump from one baby to two. You're prepared in so many ways and not in so many other ways. For me, I still wanted to do everything—be a great mum, wife, and friend, cook wonderful suppers, play educationally stimulating games with the big girl, put her to bed and all of the frills of maintaining a life with just one. The ever-changing nap schedule and routine of a newborn meant this was going to be unachievable. This will make you feel like you are sinking, but once again, no-one tells you this. Why? This is real life at its rawest, and it should be talked about. Every element of your life changes in the blink of an eye, and the nine months of knowing and getting ready for this still doesn't help. Sitting on the sofa feeding for as long as it takes when you know there is always someone else wanting you is a feeling that is indescribable, and for many, it is embraced, savoured and enjoyed. And for some of us, me, you find it incredibly hard to sit and be in the moment. I have become a lot more comfortable with this, however I could always improve that's for sure. Looking back now, what an excuse (shouldn't use that word but unsure what to use in its place). Hindsight is a wonderful thing. It's a juggle day in and day out, battling with the basics to the biggest of things that aren't really that big really, like why I didn't buy more nappies when I was out.

Talk, share, and enjoy motherhood with others, or if you're like me, write it down and moan to anyone (normally work colleagues, they have nowhere to run) about your day or night, the highs and the lows. There is normally someone willing to listen. Moreover, the newborn and older child juggle, which resembles a shit show, fixes itself—a new routine **AKA** life kicks in. That's when we should all stop and give ourselves a high five, but we don't. We just continue forth waiting for the next phase and hoping this one will be one that we sail through.

A little note to thy self: If your life is not what you want it to be right now, how can you make that change? Never rely on anyone else. My girls understand that value. I have a brain, and the internet now gives us every opportunity out there to learn any skill we want for free. Skill up in those moments you have, be it five minutes here and 10 minutes there, they all add up.

As time moves on, and that's a guarantee, when your life becomes your own again, you will know what to do with it. This is all coming from someone who lost their identity for a while. Headfirst into the Bub being my full-time job, I was stuck in that world where time ran away and so did every brain cell I had worked for. I have vowed to myself, and I am only accountable to myself, that I will write this book. I will read and learn new skills, languages, Geography, and get better at Maths. I will do that for me and only me.

Phase nineteen: The school run

I simply wanted to have this in here because for all of us the morning is vastly different, but the end game is still the same. Get them through the gates before the gates close and the shameful front entrance to reception is thrust upon you. Before I realised the 5am club, there was a manic 40 minutes to do and get everything done, which I'll discuss in a moment. I have always left for work before the girls and the hunk woke up. It has been a small price to pay for working a little bit further. Not going to lie, I hit the jackpot when I could simply leave out their breakfast and skip off to work. God, that sounds awful doesn't it? And when I read through each phase of this book, I have had to chunk out moments in my day to write to you. The time has been during my extended early morning get up that begins at 5am with no excuses. I nearly went for 4:50 but I just couldn't brave it. These chunks of time have allowed me to get this done, chunk by chunk, phase by phase. More of my wacky morning routine as we get to the end of this book.

Back to the school run.
Let me ask you, are you a get up with plenty of time on your hands kind of parent or do you leave it to the last minute and even take the toothbrushes and hairbrushes into the car to avoid any chance of landing late at that school gate? When I do the school run, I can at times be a mix of all, but being a teacher by trade, it doesn't reflect very well if I come moseying in just as the iron gates slam shut in my face. But there is always some sort of dash. My number one motto that I share with only myself (and now you) is their memory of getting ready to school was always a calm and pleasant one. I don't want theirs or my

first moments of the day to be stressed and shouty, so that has meant prepping the night before, making sure uniforms and bags are ready, lunchboxes or snacks planned and prepped if they can be. I have to admit I like the lunches fresh, so I'm a sucker and get up early to prep whatever they may be having, but I never deviate from the preplanned list of lunch and snacks I have put together, making the whole thing a robotic exercise. Moreover, the moment covid did one, we were straight back to school dinners and a bag of crisps slung in the bag as we slam the front door.

Who walks, scoots, or cycles to school? Or do you drive? Either way, there is an element of disaster at some point along the very short route to the school. It could be the weather has decided to stick its middle finger up at you and open the heavens when the skies were blue as you left. Maybe something has been forgotten (three out of five times this will happen). Or traffic! Parking and trying to park without hitting, bumping, or cursing at a fellow parent you'll have to see the moment you get out or near the gates. We have a play park right near our school, so getting stuck in there without a tantrum as we leave and onlookers gasping to see how my reaction will go down. This all being said, I have been informed on multiple occasions the hunk has no problem at all with the school run and enjoys the mornings with them. He wishes he could do it every day. I say no more. Internally, the rage is soaring. I calm myself down by simply saying, give birth and then we'll talk.

Note to self: Never concern yourself with the mild undertones of fellow parent looks, judgments, get them through the gate and concern yourself with the people that make you smile when you have left them. You don't have to be best friends with anyone or everyone in your child's class, that's not how we work or sustain the good ones that our Childs class luck has led us too.

My one thing I would say is, calm and cool mornings set them up for the day, let them know they're loved, and give them plenty of time to sloth about. If they eat breakfast, great. If not, pack an extra something in their bag for break time. It's never far away, and plenty of water, don't forget the water! These are little hacks I've found to help us along the way. Each day will never be perfect, and don't try to make it so. It's only the school run. There's plenty more important stuff we have to contend with than that and many more school runs to get it 'your' right!

Phase twenty: Going back to the grind (work)

It was 10 months into the Bub when I returned to work, and the first day was tough. The Bub had been my life's work for the past 10 months, and now, I was leaving it. Daunted, nervous, scared, and frustrated all fled into my consciousness when I left home all alone to begin a new phase for me. I pulled myself together and quietly shut the front door. Hurried down the lift and into the summers sun.

I have to say I didn't look back.

Eating my lunch in peace with both hands, chatting uninterrupted and walking around without pushing a pram or holding a small human felt exhilarating, just what the doctor ordered! When you ask the Bub do you remember mum's first day back at work she looks to me as if I've gone mad. We do all these things like prepare loving meals in our absence, stimulating activities, park play dates and the rest. They won't remember any of it. How Mum dashed home to just be with you, you may not remember but I do and that's enough. It's just the way it is.

My days back at work gradually increased until I reached four days a week and that remained. The mum guilt would always kick in at the end of the day, praying the trains would all line up and there would be no delays. So, I could get home as quickly as possible.

Back to work and those nights you would rather forget. When your child becomes unwell as the evening unfolds and you know what's in store, now that's another story.

Calling in sick to tell your boss your child is sick, and you can't come in today. Let's not forget you've had barely any sleep and actually could bullshit and just say you're sick, but you go down the other route. Of course, what can they say but are you near the phone? Are you contactable? Check your emails. However, if the boss at the other end of the line happens to be a parent as well, then most of the time a reassuring response will occur. Is this not just a crazy world we live in? Your word can sometimes just not be enough. If only they knew you would much rather get a good night's sleep and wake up to an alarm, a shower alone. Actually, the choice to go to work would most of the time be a yes, unlike so many others who would use every line under the sun to get out of work. Us mums, well in my case at least, would happily hot foot it to work if only to get a break from all the commotion back at the ranch. Adult commotion for a few hours can sometimes be just what is needed for all.

Never feel guilty for taking a day off to look after your child. They are more important than any email or work call. They won't always ask for us when they're sick, and we won't always be there to comfort them. But while we can, take it and hold onto it for as long as you can. Because sometimes momma will only do, and I am more than ok with that. Receiving another useless, time-wasting email or reminder to a meeting that could have been said in a conversation or two lined email is time wasted, and really, I'm all about savouring my time, using it, and devouring it with things, people, and bubbas that just want cuddles all day on the sofa. Yeah, I'm down with that.

What does that even look like anymore. Returning to work if this is something you needed to do like myself because you needed to go and pay back in a sense your time off, which the world thinks this is, and so we just return to work to justify the maternity leave we have just received. Why can't you receive this leave and if your circumstances change and you feel going back to work is not for you anymore you don't need to? Instead, we just return. Now for me, I reduced my teaching days to two wonderful escapes from motherhood. My return to work was a return to freedom, and I loved every minute. I could walk back into school and not deal with all the bureaucracy but simply teach and laugh with my mates. There was a ton of guilt that went with this, but I enjoyed every moment.

Phase twenty-one: The gap

The question on all their lips. The gap and how big you should go. Why is it once you seem to have your shit together, the next question asked by anyone, and everyone is: so, when are you having your next? This normally only gets asked after your first. People get bored after the second and move on! The gap is another thing everyone has an opinion on, including myself. I have an opinion now which is completely different to the one I had six years ago. The hunk and I never discussed a second child until one day we did. All we needed to do was utter the words, and another human was growing.

The reason we decided to have another child (not because the Bub asked for a sibling nope) was because the house was feeling quiet, and we needed some life kicked back into it. And sure as hell, this was the case when the bear arrived! But our gap was one month shy of six years. The hunk would have done it sooner he says, but for me, the thought of having another baby in the standard European gap of two to two and a half years sent shivers down my spine. I wasn't brave enough. Moreover, when that time arrived and the constant 'when are you having your next,' 'you have to,' 'you make such cute babies,' I simply said we are sticking to one. I need to just pause for a minute and say that for all those people that kept on asking when when when.

Amongst all the gaps, and wakes up, super early nights when CBeebies hasn't even started (UK) We do finally get there when, believe it or not, you have to wake them up! The Bub and the Bear are at very different stages as you know. I have the Bub turning 11 very soon and the bear who is turning five. I ask this question to myself often, especially when I find myself trapped in the car with them and the only way they seem to be able to communicate with each other is through the avenues of screaming and shouting. My question is, and I don't mind saying it, 'Why don't they all just stop!' During those dark and frustrating moments, all I care about is being as far away from the moaning Minnies!

We stopped at two. A very different two.

If you do run down the same rabbit hole as us and go for the second, it won't be the same. It shouldn't be the same, and that's just how it should be, but we do know with the second we will sleep again, we will eat with two hands again, and we will live to tell the tale. Now, if you are like a great friend of mine who hurtled even further down the rabbit hole and made five humans. I've got nothing for you, you're on your own with that!

Phase twenty-two: Weekends

When they were weekends.
They have so many different sides to them, and if you are reading this without any screaming children running wild in your house, then your weekend is I'm sure one of uninterrupted peace, and peace you have planned. Where lie ins are beyond 7am, lazy breakfasts mean lazy breakfasts and not just cereal thrown into a bowl, hot coffee consumed over flaky croissants, and weekend papers. Hours spent sitting in one spot. Then, a conversation about the plans and the decisions you'll make as to where to go, and it will be your decision, if and when you move from your current spot. Oh, and maybe some classical music in the background, and not the holler of another argument about who's bowling the damn ball in some Nintendo switch game.

You for sure won't have the floor is lava theme song going off in the background for the 100th time! I'm sure you are thinking of turning your life upside down; hence, you have me in your hand. One piece of advice: do not under any circumstances take what you have now for granted, no matter how much you yearn for a tiny human. It will happen in whatever format you choose, just enjoy your peace and home as it is now, or until you finish this page, enjoy it for you deserve it, or enjoy it for all those parents that would give a limb to be in your seat, if not just to sip on a hot cup of coffee.

The after weekends.
A weekend differs so much from a newborn to a toddler to a teenager. They have unwavering similarities and subtle differences. I am currently at the stage where one child would happily stay in her bedroom all day, and food is just sent up to

her. The other would like to find any form of equipment, child friendly or not, and destroy it, just destroy it whilst making as much mess and noise as possible. Polar opposites they are, but we have got to a stage where the Bear can operate her iPad and we can have some form of a lie in. Unless she doesn't know where I am, she will sit calmly in this zombified stupor for a good while, well until the battery dies!

Does anyone else dread the weekends and the position they may take? Saturday mornings can begin with a calm wakeup call or a holler, which is never a good thing. From the moment tiny humans entered our world, sleep at the weekends became a distant memory. The hunk would continue to dream, whilst I pulled my body out of the warmth and lusciousness of bed. The weekend mornings, early on were times of play and TV. The good intentions to get out the house doors early were dismissed usually due to the weather, and a lot of times due to not being arsed! Are you still in the phase of planning your weekends around nap time? If so, I kind of envy you, but I kind of don't. You feel a little stuck, especially if you did what we did and set ourselves a trap of particular sleep conditions which meant being at home and in her bed. She would not take a nap in her pram out and about. The bear being the second child would take 40 winks wherever and whenever because she just had to. Those moments of peace, of weekend bliss, disappeared as quickly as they arrived. The Bear dropped her naps very early on around a year and a half, which was harrowing and led to tantrum filled episodes about absolutely anything and a lot of the time anything that I didn't have a clue, which angered her more! The challenge of a Saturday was trying to figure out what was wrong and trying to get it to stop. As we all know, or are yet to find out, at this age, bribery doesn't work. You are left to ride the tantrum torrent for as long as it may take.

I can on one hand name the amount of times we went out for breakfast, filled our weekends with adult led activities. Our lives centred around one and then around two little beings. Only now, 11 years on and creeping into our forties, we are getting our lives back and doing bits and pieces for us. Believe me, the weekends during our thirties were anything but action packed and certainly only a few were for us and if they were, you guessed it, they were for big events, weddings, and birthdays.

It is a vicious cycle and I want to get off, but I want to stay on. Most of the time, I scrabble between needing some me time and needing the beasts around me. I write this phase whilst they both scramble around during one of their many bjj classes the hunk gets them doing, and thank god he doesn't just let them quit. They are slowly mastering a craft, an art and understanding that can't just quit when things get hard.

Whatever your weekend ends up being, hold onto the glimmers of calm or craziness that prevails. "Calmness of the mind is one of the beautiful jewels of wisdom… the more tranquil we become the greater our success." —James Allen. His collection of thoughts is just marvellous. If only I had found him earlier to dive into or hold onto when the two queens of the house screamed and shouted their way through the days.

Sibling love—there is very little of that as I write to you all now. They rarely get on with each other, and when they do, it lasts for only a few moments and it's normally because they've been given some junk to eat and actually can't argue due to their mouths being full! Did you decide to have more than one? I know we have chatted about this in previous phases, but I think it is really important to go back to it, if only briefly. I grew up in a house where there were six of us. I am the eldest with a nine-year difference between me and my youngest sister. I vowed that if I had children there would be space for them—their own bedroom to run away into and take a deep breath within. And that's exactly what we did. Two children and a bedroom each, unless they wanted to have sleepovers together, which has never happened. We all need our sanctuaries—spaces that are just for us, and the sibling love has not always been evident, but once they've had time to cool off from one another, I've noticed they seem to be able to cope a little better. The gap they have is big, but apart from looking so alike, they are polar opposites in everything they do and are. This bodes well for the future and helps immensely at times, but my God, why can't they just share! If only children understood that if they just played nicely, Mum and Dad would give them anything to keep them that way.

All we ask for is a little peace and quiet and not only when they've fallen asleep.

Let's take a side note here. It's been a week since I last wrote here which hasn't bothered me, and I'll tell you why in a moment. But now that I sit down and type, I remember the reasons why I'm doing this, and they all circle back to why I hadn't been writing in here. LIFE got in the way—good bits of life and some grotty bits, but they took me away from my goal, and now I'm behind my goal, grafting at it again. Has this pause affected my end goal? No. Will I catch up on all the sentences I have yet to write? Hell yeah! Life does get in the way of dreams and goals and targets, but drive, resilience, and the willingness to succeed will overcome all those barriers and push through. When there's no-one else around to cheer you on, this is when you must carry on. This was a pep talk to myself when I would have preferred these extra 10 minutes in bed, but hey, it's for the cause! For you and for me, to tell a story of highs and the lows.

Back to why I stopped in the first place. Firstly, sore throats and colds hit our home hard. Energy, fleeting. Sleep was king. There you go! Secondly, the Bear's fifth birthday rolled around, and I—decided to host a 20-child strong party at our house and put three hours on the invite. Yep, not the standard two-hour party drop off window, but three hours of babysitting their children, so as some of the mums chirpily mentioned on their way out, off to get a massage or a lazy breakfast. Oh, and the best, 'Could mine stay a little longer? We've booked to hang out with some friends for a brunch and drinks?' The answer to that question was a solid no. So, that took up any energy I had, along with her actual birthday the following day.

Bringing your A game is an absolute must. And the final reason that I can remember, my school had an inspection. If you're a teacher or even if you're not, imagine this: the place you are working in is being audited, inspected by three strangers with clipboards, and they're watching your every move, before, during and after office hours. Oh, it's been a week! Next weekend is mine, all mine, before the commencement of Christmas and the Bub's 11th birthday prep begins! Does it ever end? I would say a solid no. The challenges and goals, errands and so forth, just become different. I'm always juggling something, just depends which child it's for.

Phase twenty-three: Lie ins

While one sleeps, the others wail.
The consensus on lie ins and who gets them and who doesn't is an interesting topic. They definitely don't mean what they used to in those university days. In the early months of parenthood getting any sleep that wasn't a stolen 40 minutes was a blessing, and the thought of a lie in wasn't even on the cards yet. But as we've spoken about before, they do finally arrive, and you do finally get some unbroken sleep—what that looks like can be very mirky. The thing is, it's just the choice of getting up or not that is brutally taken away from you and only now with the Bub who is nearing 11 do I need to wake her up. That's a hell of a lot of missed lie ins due to being woken by a scream, crash, shake, or jump on head situation. The Bear can sometimes get to 7am, but I find that my body clock is so tuned into an early start I'm normally rousing around that time anyway of a weekend, so off I go to begin the day. Who wakes in the night when their child makes a single flinch? Yes, me too, especially in the early days. The Bub would be in our bedroom and the only way we could get her to sleep then was in a pram. Yep, you heard me. For the first I'd say six weeks of her life, she slept in a pram and all that money we spent on bassinets and cribs was wasted. Of course, being the first child, we bought the best we could afford but mini versions, so they only lasted a few months, and we'd have to go out and buy more. Fools. Second time that mistake and many others were avoided.

Going back to the sleep. She slept in a pram after her milk feed and top up. She would rarely wake because every time she moved or made any noise, I'd wake. What is that? Mother's intuition? Guess who doesn't wake at all? Yep, the hunk who is right next to said noise. Eleven years on, I still get this ball of nerves in the pit of my stomach when I sense one of them is going to be unwell. That's at least one of my nights of sleep gone out the window! Who do they want in the hour be it 2am, 4am, or 6am? Yep, you ladies know it... Mumma! But if there are any men reading this or happen to pick the book up and it falls to this page, do this, no matter how tired you are. That woman has been up most of the night tending to your children, maybe even feeling run down herself, but she must continue on, exhausted, so do the courtesy of realising this before the shit hits the fan over the most minor thing and give her a damn lie in! And don't just sit on the sofa and let them tear around the place, take them out and let her sleep and rest her weary head. You never know when you'll need those bonus points again!

Phase twenty-four: Getting your me back

What a rabbit hole this is.
Where to start? As you are aware, I'm 11 years into this thing they call parenting, and I still don't think I have my life fully back yet. I still feel the guilt when I go and do something for myself. Actually, I'm currently writing this after the Bear woke up super early with a stomachache, which I think is just an excuse to get up early and get her iPad. So, this typing sesh will be short. My thirties have been pretty much solely dedicated to my children. Everything I have done has been for them, and a big part of me was lost at times. However, a new me was built and grew out of these last 11 years, which writing this and thinking about all that, I realise that during parenthood you lose your identity. You just become Mum, but the days where you are you and you are surrounded by people who call you by your name can be magical.

Work for me in the early days as I've mentioned before was a life saver! I laughed more in that department than I had done for a long time! I don't think the jokes were any funnier, the people were any jollier, or we suddenly became comedians overnight. I think the crux of it was I was able to be me, Victoria, and not anyone or anything else. I adored those part time days of dipping in and out of work and dashing back to hang out with the bub, who had no idea I had left at all.

Side note: If you take one thing from this book, (I've said this before I know, but I feel this is a goody) your children won't remember when you ask them to think back to all the times you risked life and death to get home to them, or when you spent freezing cold mornings, afternoons, and evenings at the park with them. Or when you bought them all that plastic they ever wanted for Christmas. If you have elder children, please go and ask them if they remember all that extra Lego building time you spent with them. Most of the time, they don't remember, it's in built and embedded and it matters, but if it doesn't happen one day that's ok. For your child It may be a vague memory, that you've had to coax out of them to remember. I'm not saying to not spend really meaningful time with them, that is deeply focused on them and only them. But don't risk everything, cancel that drink or date night because you may miss one or two bath times or stories at bed. These are all the little things I wish someone had told me. Your children will be fine.

Instead, have starry nights, glitzy cocktails, even if just the one, lie ins which you don't feel guilty about, horizontal days on the sofa, home days where they have to entertain themselves, screen days, and mum reading a book days. These all count and are meaningful life moments that cannot and shouldn't be saved for when they are grown up. We should not be clawing our lives back after 10 or so years. We should have our life in between theirs, all together.

My main aim as Mum was always for the girls to think back to a childhood of smiles, good times spent together, moments of doing nothing, laughter, open conversations, and everything else that life throws into the mix. Not this grumpy Mum who cleaned the house all day, never sat and played a game of cards, never laughed and listened and escaped the craziness when she needed to. I want them to look back and understand it was their childhood, but it was also Mum and Dad's life as well. We had growth in there, and we shared it together.

Laughter and time spent together, that's it really. If they have that and it's the core of everything, then I think we've cracked it! Oh, and Mum told said to never be a sheep, don't follow others, be yourself and if that's not good enough, then tell them in the nicest possible way to buggar off!

A glimmer. It's the little things that count. I started

training people after the Bear, offering workouts and a place for the children to go. Working with other Mums and doing something productive, helped immensely with getting some ownership over my time again. Not Mum, but entrepreneur Victoria for a time had a revolving door of mums coming in for a workout. However, missing the routine that leaving for work gave was the ebb to my flow, and so I went in search of some working in a school once more. The freedom of searching for a new job, using the grey matter again that gets left behind in the early stages of parenthood, was to be flexed again, to be used, challenged. That is, I think, a bloody important part of getting your life back. I never questioned who I was after having the girls, but I did question where I had gone.

Phase twenty-five: More food

No matter what stage you are with your child, they still need feeding, be it milk from the boob, bottle, or the hard stuff. It happens every day, sometimes all day, and it is very much talked about and judged! As I have mentioned way back in the early phases of this rollercoaster life they call parenting, I switched to formula very early on with the Bub and lasted a few months with the bear before we switched. There were a few reasons with the Bub, mainly surrounding the fact my nipples were falling off and the pain was too much to bare, and to top it off, the sleepless nights hit me like a ton of bricks. I switched to formula and paired it with breast for Bear as I wanted to get my life back a bit. I had heard horror stories (here we go again with the stories) that some babies don't take the bottle and only want the boob.

Let's chat about introducing solids into your baby's diet and what a fucking mess that can be, an absolute minefield of underfeeding and over feeding and smoothies, organising green blends and frozen or reheated delights. They both ate better than me and the hunk combined until I reconsidered all the time spent doing the prep and decided they will just eat what we eat, minus the vindaloos and coffee (and for me, wine)! Things became a little easier, but I still had no clue how much to give against the milk or if she was getting too much or too little. So, the milk ended up being the sustenance needed for me to ensure she got enough. There are so many books out there, so many discussions about what to give and what not to give. We are all fully aware that a burger and chips versus the ole faithful broccoli is going to lose. I would just once like to see some of those mums back in the day if I just happened to mention that last night the bub sank a McDonald's Big Mac meal and followed it up with a bottle of milk. Oh, they would have a field day! (I'm joking)

We know what they should and shouldn't be eating, but sometimes, all you have the energy to cook is a pesto pasta. Believe me, my kids survived on pesto pasta, the Monday-Friday staple, for many months! Fridays would be treats and the weekend could be a free for all. I get that there are so many ways we can fail when it comes to fueling our kids, and that's what it is a lot of the time. Fuel. To keep them legging it around your 2-bed apartment or jumping off the nearest death trap. But I am also a crazy headstrong advocate of the good stuff, and I have one that would eat broccoli until the cows come home and another who has obviously been doing her homework and prefers a raw veg diet! But if you do want a cheeky win that I see no child turn their snotty nose up at (that is in the literal sense!), then try crispy kale. Get a tray, drizzle olive oil, and get some good salt. Mix and bake until crispy. This my friends is a win, and if you already know this, then I'm sure you'd agree with me. I'll pop some food ideas at the back of this book, just in case.

Side note: It is true what they say, you are what you eat and eating a colourful diet is key. Oily fish, green veggies, berries galore, and loads of water. Sometimes, and maybe days on end, that just isn't happening for you or them, but don't go comparing yourself to anyone else. Instead, realise that isn't how it always is and longingly look back on that one day she or he ate a carrot without spitting it out (ok maybe more than one day). What I'm trying to say is there are always, always days where noodles from a bag and a packet of biscuits will do, and that's it. That's fine with me! God, I look back to what we grew up on, well at least for me, and I remember those turkey drummers that came from the freezer. I have to say I loved freezer night. We could pick anything we liked from the freezer and heat it up! Those were the days, securely lodged in my memory banks. Of course, I also remember the home cooked lasagnas and shepherd's pies, but the freezer night, that's a night I now do with my family!

Phase twenty-six: Traditions

I wasn't sure if I should include this, then I remembered how much I love traditions and all the little and big things we do that hopefully will stick with them. Come on, we all have a tradition. It may not be singing around a roaring campfire as we all play a musical instrument, but there's always at least one in there. From the Saturday breakfast all together, even if it's in between a device or two (anything so I can down a few croissants in peace) to the tooth fairy or opening presents in bed, going on a bike ride, Sunday movies, cooking in the kitchen, or whatever it maybe, I'm a staunch believer in them and the goodness they bring out in all of us. So, here's a list of my family's traditions, and if you fancy it, find my email at the back of the book. I would love you to share a fave family tradition you did as a child and have carried forward or one you created for your family now.

Let's start with the standard ones: Tooth fairy. (Look away children who can read!)

Does she forget on occasions and make some utter of corkers of excuses the next day? Yes, she does! I have a classic story of this one. I still to this day believe it was not my fault and was actually my nine-year-old daughter's at the time. So of course, I follow along and don't leave a note, just a coin. Oh Jesus, what a mistake this was! Calls and messages on my phone while I'm at work. The Bub is beside herself and now thinks the tooth fairy doesn't exist! The hunk is making all sorts of excuses about why she did that. I'm confused and then also follow along with this string of lies, when really it's my daughter's whole issue, but let's not go there. From what I can remember, all was fine in the end, and I do believe a letter appeared and the said mistake was never repeated. Jesus, but the bloody tooth fairy and all that goes with it is a task that only a reminder on the phone can fix.

Who else started the bloody Elf on the damn shelf? It looked so fun and effortless, especially when you scroll through bloody Pinterest with all those wonderful normally American mothers (btw they are queens of all of this, be it festivities, birthdays, creative minds on some sort of celebration, they have it down to an art). I didn't mean to generalise, but it's for all to see—they are goddesses on that damn Pinterest! Back to the main story and the Elf. We first started with one, then there was two, and now, the Bub said why don't we have a girl? So muggins here has just spent £20 on a pink girl elf, basically the same as the other two but dressed in pink. The December juggle is real in my household, because I want to do it all, but my bank balance says otherwise. I'm not one of those people that can fashion homemade garlands, wreaths, and homegrown gifts. I'm just about managing a few Christmas trees with air dry clay. This all being said, the elves if you're not aware must come and hide in different spots every night in December. Ours normally arrives as late as possible or when I'm fed up with the girls asking, "Where's whizzy and bubbles?" Yes, they have names. Oh, this could take some time! Settle in guys, and if you are dealing or have dealt with said elves, then you may nod along or laugh as I recount.

They should arrive every evening and cause havoc with the premise of watching over your children for good behaviour. If behaviour is not good, they report back to Santa and tend to not move from the night before. This is gold dust because if you're anything like me, forgetting to move the elf or even find it after you've hidden somewhere that during your mad haste to remove the elves has now gone missing! The creativity of some of the escapades these elves get up to is another level of parent amazingness. I've seen some scenes that Martin Scorsese would stand back in awe at. For me, if I can get them laced up and hung from a ceiling somewhere I've done well. The competition is fierce, and the Instagram pages are stacked full of inspiration, but if your children don't ask and you want to keep your December nights horizontal on a sofa, then don't fall into the Pinterest, school mum at the gate content. Enjoy your peace because secretly we're all wishing we had ignored it all as well.

There are many other mini traditions or events that happen through sheer luck; Sunday lounging breakfast with some board games or a game of Uno thrown into the mix. This doesn't happen every weekend, like this one just gone. Instead, they were glued to their screens, and I didn't have the energy to get them off, so we sat and had the odd chat in between YouTube ad breaks. But when that one happens, it's a goody! Fish and chip Friday, no need to explain this one, dates back to my childhood and is too bloody delicious to not continue. Halloween of course. Birthdays with Stevie Wonder belting out in the background. Pancakes and yummy home cooked din dins, sometimes it's freezer Thursdays and Fridays, but a lot of the time, it is a one bake dish which are always winners! There are more I'm sure intertwined into our hectic days, but those are the ones my memory is deciding to put on paper at this moment in time!

Phase twenty-seven: Friends

Those friends they didn't want as your friends, will you repeat with yours? Do you ever remember your mum or dad having a question or two about your choice of friend? They weren't that keen on your being mates and had many, many things to say about it! I had one of those said friends for only a short space of time, and we shared the same first name, but that was the only thing we had in common from what I can remember. I vaguely recall going around to my new buddy's place and serving her mum a cup of tea and finding food in the freezer to eat, no interaction from her mum which I found odd, but what I didn't find odd and absolutely loved was being able to choose my supper and from a chest freezer that happened to be rammed through of beige frozen goodness! Along with that surprise, we were then taken around their farm on a questionable Land Rover that jolted to a stop and banged my head into the dashboard, giving me a nosebleed and my mum the evidence she needed to cancel that friendship for good, along with some rather heated words with the mum, who still remained seated on her sofa for the entirety of my one and only visit.

What are your thoughts on friends that are questionable? I have had a couple of incidences where a parent has had a side word about one of mine, and hats off to me for keeping a cool head. The friends you wouldn't pick for your child, but you have no choice, depending on age, most of the time they ride the storm, and everything turns out ok. Until the birthday party or play date conversations come up, if that friendship is still going strong and the thought of sitting on some awkward play date with a parent who you have nothing in common with is on the cards, you need to as subtle as you can start to wean your child off this friend, by any means necessary. I have a friend that did just this, and she blamed the issue on allergies—nothing more was said! Allergic to what I'm not sure, and never asked. There is always, always a solution to anything, it's just finding it and making it work, that's where the problem lies. A sneaky whisper in a teacher or helper's ear has never done any harm! Get someone else to have those awkward conversations I say is the way forward.

If you are nowhere near these kinds of situations yet and are still contending with the initial phases of parenthood, some of us are looking on your life quite enviously. The grass is not always greener, and every phase of parenthood throws up its own challenges. It's navigating those without too much judgement of oneself and others has to be the only way forward. I'm no guru or self-help know it all. I'm a full-time working woman with a couple of humans I so happen to keep alive, smiling, fed, and clothed on a daily basis. That being said, it's the bloody Christmas party. I've got no festive fucking treats, the Christmas t-shirts didn't arrive from Amazon, and they wanted packed lunches today. Oh, and to top it off, the damn elves need to arrive today, and I can't bloody find them!

Phase twenty-eight: When it's all said and done

When it's all said and done and the day draws to a close, try to look back on everything you have achieved, whether it be big or small. Making a cup of coffee for me back when the Bub was small and drinking it warm would put a smile on my face, and that was my small win. Remember my wins may not be the same as yours but they are still a win however you look at them.

List the wins here:

1.
2
3.
4.
5.
6.
7.
8.
9.
10.

For you, for your family, for your friends, for your work. Whatever it is, acknowledge it (God, that sounds like a self-help book). Anyway, scribble it, take a moment and realise I'm shit hot, I get stuff done, even if my list never ends, there were things I ticked off and that means I'm winning somewhere and that's good for me. Moreover, there will always be days where you just don't tick that list, and that's also ok. I promise you there will be a small win in there somewhere though, you just have to find it.

As this book draws to a close, I find myself sitting here after hosting my Bub's 11th birthday party. That's a win and probably something I'll forget to tick off my list. We did a sleepover, and my win was that, a sleepover where she chose the bedtime, the music and the friends. A win that only a small portion of the population choose to do every day. My daily biggest wins are firstly I got up, stretched, drank my lemon and water, took my prebiotics, walked, and I sat and typed to you. That's my win for today. Even if nothing else comes to pass I know that I've done a couple of things already. If you're reading this and starting out all of this maybe unfamiliar, unrealistic and damn right off topic, if you take one thing from all of the above let it be this.

Celebrate the small wins—the high days where more sleep happened, you ate a meal uninterrupted, the baby latched, drank milk, and there was minimal screaming and crying from all parties! You had some time alone with your other half, you managed to reply to a message or two. These are wonderful things. Understand that, take a breath and give yourself a solo high five!

For you and me. When you're feeling low, come and say hello. A reminder to yourself that you are never alone.

I thought I would jot down some quotes that I've kept with me on scrap bits of paper, in my bag, on the fridge, bathroom mirror and everywhere in between. Use them or don't but I have to say if you're having a bad day or even an utterly fabulous day and a kick up the arse is what's needed, then read on, take what you need, bookmark, and hopefully one sticks with you, and you take that along with you. There are too many wonderful words of wisdom I could have added here, but instead, I jotted down all the ones I use often, reflect my values and lifestyle, and really just make me get my shit together. Hope there's some words of wisdom in here for you too.

"Calmness of the mind is one of the beautiful jewels of wisdom. The more tranquil you become the greater our success." —James Allen

(This one is stuck down on my laptop. I should definitely look at it more than I do!)

"Difficulty is what we do. Don't compare yourself to people who don't have the purpose you have. Difficulty doesn't kill who you are, it reveals who you are." —Eric Helmes

(This quote is from one of his podcasts, and it helped a lot in the really tough days. The juggle was very much real as I've mentioned before. These kinds of strong, powerful and get your fucking self-sorted woman quotes help a lot!)

"A winner is a dreamer that never gives up. It's difficult to follow your dreams, you have to follow your dreams or someone else will hire you to build theirs."

(Oh, how true. This one is just powerful to its core.)

"How strong is your why? You have to show up even when no-one is supporting you, no-one is watching you, you have to keep going, you have to work, day in day out. You can't build a six pack by doing one set of crunches."

(When all I wanted to do was have a lie in and not deal with the world around me, this lady got me out of bed and focused on whatever shit needed to be done, and that shit at the time was this, me writing to you.)

"Self-discipline, those who succeed are not fearless; they had to show up, do the work behind the scenes, make things happen when others would not. It's doing within when you're doing without. A student is resilient, a student is consistent, a student is a dreamer who never gave up."

"Every dream requires discipline. Your potential is endless; now go do what you set out to do."

"Not every day is promised; don't forget that."

"Self-discipline is the difference between success and failure."

And finally, one from me:

"Take your dreams seriously, no matter how big or small, and never lose sight of them."

Here are 10 go-to food ideas I have used time and time again to keep them going.

Don't beat yourself up about this, don't compare, judge or worry. Food is food, as I've said before. Not every day is filled with beige, carb ridden, refined sugar stacked, but some days it is, and that is bloody fine. But on the days you do have a little extra energy, or there's a few vegetables that need using up, here's some quick hacks I've used over the years that may help or may not. Share with a friend, eat with friends, and if you're offered a playdate, carefully time it over a lunch or tea, so it's one less meal to think about (you didn't hear that from me).

Krispy Kale
Tear up some washed kale. Add around 1 tbsp olive oil

and 1/2 tsp of good quality salt mix with hands until leaves are coated. Then, pop it into a preheated oven around 180c and bake for 10-12 minutes or until crispy. My girls love love love this snack.

Toasties

Ok this is an obvious one, but it can be a win for a quick lunch/tea or brekkie.

I use sourdough, thinly sliced, and I add good cheddar and a chutney or pickle. I put some green normally carvel in the middle, which they normally miss, add some salami and a good grind of salt and pepper. Toast up and serve. Good luck!

Potatoes or glorious potato chips:

For speed, I peel the potatoes and slice thinly and bung it on a baking tray. Then, wash the potato skins and put in a separate baking tray. Add olive oil and salt and pepper to both trays and bake the potato skins for 15-20 minutes. The potato chips bake for around 35-40 minutes. Give them a good shake and mix to get them all crispy and yummy. Serve up with some raw veggies or something fruity!

Pancakes:

I mean come on. I remember my mum used to do savoury, sweet, plain, and anything else she could find. Cheap and easy, and it can't help but put a smile on your face.

I love the big fluffy ones, so here's an all-in-one bowl beast of a recipe.

Sling 3 cups of self-rising flour in a bowl with 1tsp of bicarb powder and mix. Add one cracked egg (never whisk before, I can never be bothered to waste time on that), and melt half a block of butter (yea, that's right). They're smiley pancakes, and they'll put a smile on anyone's face! Mix, then add a pinch of good salt, 1-1.5cups of whole milk and stir until it meets a thick consistency. Melt a little butter in a pan and spoon in the cakes. Cook until brown, give them a pat and make sure the batter is spongy. Once spongy, stick whatever you fancy on top, or let them do that! Hey ho, and there's another plate of food ticked off the list.

Cheese and biscuits

Does exactly what it says on the tin, and this is something I do often for a tea after a club or as a snack. A kiddie friendly cheesy board, if you will. Cut up what you have with veggies, fruit, and bung it in the middle of the table and let them serve. For smaller Bubs, pop on their tray nice and small, and leave the biscuits or maybe give them one or two to suck on. Don't change things up. Keep things simple. Don't make more work for yourself. Life is too bloody short!

Peanut butter and jam sarnie

This is childhood in one bloody delicious melty, oozy, crunchy deliciousness. Get yourself some thick white bread, sourdough or whatever you have. The thicker the slice for me the better. Layer up the peanut butter (your choice), then jam it up—again, your choice. Now in a pan add some butter and allow it to melt. Make sure it's nice and hot, then add the sandwich. Let it get brown and crispy on one side, then flip over. Yep, we know this is going to be insane. Once crispy and brown, pop on some kitchen roll, cut, and devour.

Pasta and tomato sauce

I will always make a tomato sauce and freeze it. This is all dependent on the energy I have that day or week, so sometimes, it doesn't even happen. Fry up a load of garlic and onion, you choose the quantity—I normally go three thinly sliced garlics and one onion, sliced as thinly as time will allow. Fry with some butter. Add some carrot, simmer down, bung in some chopped tomatoes—around six cherry tomatoes and a couple of large ones, if I have them. Add two tinned tomatoes chopped and some water, 1 tbsp of honey or sugar, and season. Simmer on a low heat for a half hour. There's your tomato sauce! Boil up some pasta, whatever you have, grate some cheese, and serve up. It never fails!

Picky board

This can be savoury or sweet, full of leftovers and cupboard crap. Something I tend to resort to on a Friday or weekend, and it normally goes down pretty well.

My holy moly me that's spicy shot of goodness

Sorry, but I've wasted enough money on premade fancy shop bought shots, I now make my own.

Ginger into the blender (4/5)
Turmeric fresh or powder (fresh 5/6 or 1tbsp)
3 lemons juiced
1tbsp apple cider vinegar
1tsp good quality salt
1 apple cut into chunks

Blitz/strain and pour a little to taste. Adjust where needed. I tend to drink a shot sized amount every morning or until we run out and I need to make more. Lemon water first and this second. There's a bit of me time right there in those two drinks, if I've got up early enough to enjoy both uninterrupted. If I haven't, then that's on me!

One more thing. I fast most days and skip breakfast, which works for me. I've got the energy I need and the black coffee I adore, puts a whacking great smile on my face and keeps me going. This is all great until the holidays come around and all the good stuff I've kept going through the term time goes out the window and the alarm clock goes off, the me time mornings and solitude disappears, again that's on me. I should keep it going, but I just love my bed too much!

Phase oh, who knows...

The phase where all the phases have kind of disappeared, and I sit here at the end of a tale that was quite simply a woman's viewpoint of the messiness that is parenthood.

As I reach this part of the book, I know I still have some way before getting it out into the world and what comes with that is a lot of self-doubt, criticism, and wonder if anyone will actually even give this the time of day. But for all it's worth, this small body of writing was written for two reasons. As I've eluded to in the pages before, I set myself a challenge to achieve some goals of my own by the time I turn 40, which is fast approaching. This mother's tale was one of them and it has been my conscious, sub-conscious, and endless thought for many, many months. The endless trudge at times where I've wanted to sit and do anything but plug away at this, but I persevered and persevered to prove a point that anything can be achieved, if you put your time and effort into it you too can be an author to more than just your children's lives, but to your own.

When all is said and done, these words, each and every one of them, has been written during my 5am wake up, my quick nip to the mall, and 10 stolen minutes here and there. I have not spent longer than 15 minutes writing this, hence it was never going to be a lengthy book, but it is merely something to be picked up and put down, because if we're truly honest, there's a lot more stuff we have to contend with, fires to put out, and glasses of wine to be poured than to spend hours and hours meandering through page upon page of another person's take of the world.

My second reason for writing this book is because of two wonderful, strong, and empowering women who I don't see as much as I'd like but who made a profound impact on me. My time spent with them fired my need to continue to write and tell my story. To you both, thank you for telling me to write down and share my truths. Well, ladies I did, and you may not remember, but at last 11 years later that moaning, winging lass has done it, and she thanks you for lighting up that flicker within me.

To end.

You may have flicked through, scanned, or even, just maybe, turned over some pages for another day. I will leave you with the following, Your life is happening now, while you read this. Everything that matters is happening right now, so make damn sure to carve some time for you. Here are some of the ways I've done just that during this decade. Some days, it's been easier than others. Some days, it's been a fucking mess, and I've had no time for me, and the demand for mum or wife has been off the charts. But when I have found that time, these are the things I've done.

I've made a point of getting up one hour earlier than anyone else. This of course only started to get woven into my daily routine when the Bub and the Bear were sleeping and a little older. I do know there are some women out there better than me that still get up at the crack of dawn and get that me time. That's just not me. I need to sleep, and if I don't get at least five to seven hours, I'm a nightmare.

The morning madness of getting the children up and everything else that goes with it begins. Keeping the house calm is fundamental and something I strive bloody hard to maintain every day. I don't think they even notice, but I always go back to what I want them to remember about their childhood and that is a happy and loving home. I think the hunk and I do a pretty good job of keeping that ship steady. Well, most of the time anyway.

Find your time, find what puts a smile on your face and repeat, repeat, repeat unless it's spending shit loads of cash you don't have on stuff that helps in the short term but solves nothing in the long term. For me, it has always been exercise, the sun, and a glass of red. What's yours? And believe me, if all else fails, stick your headphones on and go for a walk, with or without the tribe.

My little escape hacks that have helped me improve as a mother, wife, friend & most importantly me. Maybe one or two might be something you already do or maybe not.

- Take a walk
- Turn the music up high and dance like everybody is watching
- Read a book that helps you feel good
- Take a breath
- Find that person who you can just vent to without needing any explanation for it
- Learn something, anything new that brings a spark to your day
- Get up early however early that is and find a moment for yourself
- Stop everything and just sit and drink a hot or cold drink whichever you prefer
- Be kind to yourself and the people YOU choose to have around you
- Eat some really good food and don't worry about the calories in any of it
- Drink water, good quality mineral rich water
- Sleep, sleep, sleep when and wherever you can

In the words of Robin Sharma, "Commit yourself to managing your time more effectively, a sense of awareness about how imprudent your time really is. Don't let people waste this most precious of commodities and invest it only in those activities that truly count."

I couldn't have said it better myself.

Bibliography

- Someday is Today—Matthew Dicks
- Goodreads—Abraham Lincoln
- As a Man Thinketh—James Allen
- Motivation Daily by Diversity—Varied
- Life Lessons From the Monk Who Sold His Ferrari — Robin Sharma

Acknowledgements

I have to start by thanking my husband, Douglas. From listening to my first thoughts before pen was put to paper, to giving me advice throughout. He has held my hand and never let go, te amo. To Emilia and Alice (Bear) this book would not be here if you two were not. Thank you for always being honest and telling me if something rocked or sucked.

Thank you to the wonderful ladies who helped this book come to life, the patience you gave me will never be forgotten. Writing a book is harder than I thought, yet more rewarding than I could ever imagined. I want you to know that what you have read has been based on the early lives of parenthood, some of it has been edited, changed and at times protected but for most of it, the tales are as true as they can be.

Finally, I would like to thank you for taking the time to invest in me and more importantly invest in you. Never forgot there was a YOU before, go now and say hi again.

One more thing, Doug, Emilia, and Alice—you are my *Ikigai*.

—Victoria Dos Santos

Printed in Great Britain
by Amazon